Six-Word Lessons for Strength-Based Business Success

100 Lessons to Build Power, Confidence and Fortitude at Work

Kate Nugent Curtis

Published by Pacelli Publishing
Bellevue, Washington

Six-Word Lessons for Strength-Based Business Success

Published by Pacelli Publishing
9905 Lake Washington Blvd. NE, #D-103
Bellevue, Washington 98004
PacelliPublishing.com

Cover and interior design by Pacelli Publishing
Cover photo by AdobeStock
Author photo by Yuen Lui Photography

ISBN-10: 1-933750-51-0
ISBN-13: 978-1-933750-51-4

Introduction

The idea of writing a book about strength, fortitude and will power was a convergence of three new endeavors in my life: a hobby, an athletic challenge and my career. In 2010 I took up blogging as a fun late-night hobby while my kids were sleeping. I decided to write about kettlebells, since they were still fairly new on the fitness scene. I created a WordPress blog titled *Kettlebell Hell* and started writing *Cast Iron Strength, thoughts about the amazing power of kettlebells.* For more than six years my entries have ranged from daily workouts, to music and food suggestions, to the occasional commentary of my strongly-held convictions.

However, something unexpected happened. After several years of swinging kettlebells, I uncovered a new strength that led me to pursue open water swimming. I was faced with a whole new set of athletic challenges ranging from storms at sea and ocean swells to hypothermia and creepy aquatic life. It was exhilarating, terrifying and absolutely wonderful all at once. Every swim taught me about perseverance and staying dedicated to something you love.

Meanwhile, as a fairly new entrepreneur, I was helping my corporate clients tackle some of their toughest communication challenges, both on stage and with the media. Inspired by what my clients were up against, I created a new program called Grounded in Strength©. Every person I've worked with has helped me understand a great deal about being human, finding your voice, working through fears and tackling job demands.

In the end, you might say that my three worlds perfectly collided to provide a unique perspective on strength and perseverance which became the impetus for writing this book. Through it all, one thing has become crystal clear to me: Where you find passion, you will find fortitude.

Every lesson in this book has been something I have experienced first-hand. Because of that, all 100 lessons are deeply personal to me. If you feel moved to want to discuss anything further, please reach out to me at kcurtis@communicationtactics.com. Thank you for reading my 100 lessons.

Acknowledgements

To my husband, Elliot Curtis, a man of great patience and wisdom, thank you for being my rock and my touchstone.

To my parents, Joan and Bill Nugent, thank you for your constant curiosity in me. It has helped me become who I am today.

To my coach, Nate Horst, thank you for your solid advice and steady confidence in my strength.

Finally, a special thanks to the entire open water swimming community across our beautiful planet. I admire each and every one of you. I find great joy in your endeavors and I am constantly motivated by your fortitude. I am so blessed to be a part of this wonderful group of people.

Dedication

To Claire and Marcus

May you both find your passion,
and thus, your fortitude.

Contents

What Does Authentic Confidence Look Like?

Start here: identify your greatest strengths.

Where do you excel and what are your greatest strengths? There is a deep reservoir of confidence waiting for you, all you need to do is acknowledge your strengths. Unfortunately, many people have never taken the time to identify their greatest strengths. Without self-knowledge, this reservoir remains untapped.

Articulate your strength to become it.

When you are able to clearly communicate your strength in a consistent and concise way, you become better equipped to draw on that strength when you need it. Get a clear mindset and then complete this sentence: "I feel strong when…" Fill in the blank with your particular expertise or skill.

Authentic confidence comes from realized goals.

Drawing on a personal strength to attain authentic confidence often starts with a goal. Set a goal, set your mind to achieve that goal, and then get after it. An accomplished goal will provide the visuals you need to reconnect with the feeling of success and will ultimately provide a greater sense of confidence.

Must be recent, personal and great!

Acknowledge your strength and then own it. But make sure it's recent. If you had to go back a number of years to dig up an old strength, reconsider what you have going on today, and how your life has changed. Challenge yourself to own a new strength today, and keep adding additional ones.

Must be accessible and easily retrievable

If you could reach into your back pocket and pull out two or three words that would offer strength, what would they be? Write them down on a slip of paper and try it. The act of doing this will allow you to retrieve your strength when you need it. Soon you won't need the paper. Visualize!

Your strength-based approach to life

Bring your authentic confidence to work every day. When you walk in the door, anchor on a past excellence and let it drive you. Bring every ounce of your previous win to your potential today. What starts as a mindful practice will soon become a natural part of how you move through the world.

Confidence is built over many years.

Confidence is defined as "firm trust." It is not arrogant, boisterous or immediate. It is a quiet certainty that develops over time. All of your experiences, accomplishments, and even failures build the foundation of your authentic confidence. Imagine yourself walking with firm trust as you enter a new situation.

Know yourself well. That is all.

The confidence that comes from truly knowing yourself is immeasurable. Through the years it has allowed me to reject other's uninformed opinions about me. That is power. Spend time understanding who you are and where your strongest convictions lie, and you will never be lost. Strong confidence in self cannot be shaken.

Never stop stepping up your game.

What does it mean to be content? Defined as a "peaceful happiness," many people strive for contentment, but it can also be seen as stagnation. A quiet, peaceful, inertia. However, if you want to step up your game, tackle new challenges, and open up to new experiences in this life, I don't think contentment is what you're looking for.

With authentic confidence, you cannot fail.

You find yourself saying "yes" instead of "no." You raise your hand and say "I'm in!" Life becomes fuller and more meaningful. You get to the point in this mind game where you know you cannot fail. Because of what you have done, you know what you can do, and what is possible. When the opportunities come, you are ready.

Borrowed from Athletes, Applied to Business

Always be in pursuit of goals.

"You are what you take time to become." This single statement has been the driving force behind the pursuit of my goals. Consider your authentic strengths, set some goals, and then make a personal commitment to push performance. Just the act of committing to a goal shows spirit and demonstrates determination in the act of doing.

The critic in the comfortable chair.

When we take on lofty goals, there will always be those who want to point out how the "strong man stumbles." Ignore them. They do not matter. Advice adopted from Theodore Roosevelt: It is not the critic in the comfortable chair who matters. Win or lose, your effort is everything. It shows guts just to be in the game.

Optimize performance in sports and business.

Athletes will perform the same motion over and over again to lock a particular movement into their neuromuscular memory. The repeated patterns help them make the movement without conscious effort, letting go of the details and allowing them to "get into the zone." Imagine optimizing this for a business presentation.

There's no zone for the novice.

"We are what we repeatedly do." But if this is your first time, do not expect to find the zone. Doing anything for the first time takes hours drilling down on fundamentals and technique. Once we form the right habits we can train our mind and body to find the zone. Always take time to perfect your craft.

Coming back stronger after a disappointment

Athletes are constantly striving to set a personal record. We celebrate by ringing a "PR bell." However, I've had weeks roll by without a ding, and in my disappointment my trainer will remind me: “You can’t PR every day!” This is also true in business. Rest and resilience will pay off, and we get stronger every time we try.

Growth where it matters: between sets

Just as training is the right combination of stress plus recovery, it's important to consider this in business as well. Quite often it's the rest between the sets that will refresh us for what's next and help us stay ready. Consider how much sleep you're getting each night, and don't let those vacation days slip away.

17

Cash in your investment of time.

In sports and business, preparation is key. Athletes prepare for months and often years for a single event. It becomes nearly impossible to second-guess yourself when you've put in the hours. Invest the time, confidence will follow. When "the hay is in the barn," your work is done. Game on: it's time to cash in your investment with confidence.

Challenge yourself, but don't compare yourself.

Push the boundaries of your own success, but don't compare yourself with others. Athletes keep personal training logs to give them the information and knowledge they need to move forward, each day building on the next. Do you have a training log for your business?

10

Acknowledge the power of the mind.

Athletes train their mind and their body. The mind is a very deep reservoir of strength. When it is important to succeed, tap the mind. Imagery will help you pull out your best performance when you need it. Learn to discipline your mind and know that persistence will pay off. Dig deep and don't give up. This is will power!

Find your passion to stay committed.

Professional athletes are not immune to challenges, but it's their passion that keeps them committed and coming back every day. When the task begins to feel like just a lot of hard work, the natural tendency will be to bail. With passion, we become committed with our heart, and find our fortitude.

Are you a specialist or generalist?

There are no generalists at the Olympics. Sure, sometimes it's fine to be a "jack of all trades," however when it's time to shine, it's time to specialize. Pull out your inherent strengths, dedicate the time, and position yourself as an expert.

Bring Strength to the Conference Room

22

Are you a spectator or contributor?

This is not a debate about introversion and extroversion. Contributing ideas is not something that's reserved just for extroverts. It's about walking into a conference room with the strength and confidence you need to become a valuable contributor. Make a commitment to add importance and interest to every meeting.

Authentic engagement comes from the heart.

"Nobody cares how much you know until they know how much you care." This insightful quote is often attributed to Theodore Roosevelt. In many meetings you'll often notice a fine line between silence and over-contributing. Observe first, then seek to understand, and finally, engage with wisdom.

Claim your right to actively participate.

Struggling to get a word in edgewise? Move something. Preferably your whole arm from your shoulder to your fingertips. Insert yourself physically into the conversation, and see how you can command attention. Knowing how to use an appropriate gesture can give you the power to be heard and will allow you to actively participate in the conversation.

Don’t be a conference room backbencher.

What’s true in Parliament is also true in the conference room! Backbenchers have little or no power. My advice? Always arrive early for meetings to get the best seat at the table. Then don't be afraid to spread out and take up space. (see next lesson)

Space at the table equals power.

Studies have shown that physical space has been associated with confidence and power. When we sit down at the table and take up more physical space (with our legs, elbows and gestures) we appear more authoritative. Think of the executive who walks around the room while talking vs. sitting. Either way, practice communicating over a broader area of space.

"Do not be afraid to interrupt."

Wise words attributed to Madeleine Albright--by all means, interrupt! Forget what you learned in kindergarten. The longer misinformation stays "out there" and unchallenged, the more believable it becomes. Women tend to take more time than men to size up a situation and respond, so this is especially good advice for the women in the room.

Sometimes silence is not always golden.

So you say you're an introvert? Once again, this is not a Myers-Briggs debate. When you're "up for bat" in a business discussion, it takes a split second for your brain to decide to speak up or defer. Think of your contribution as a performance. Anyone can "bring it" for a short period of time.

Perseverance: a fancy word for grit.

Business meetings can definitely raise your levels of cortisol (a stress hormone) and increase your overall anxiety. This is when business fortitude becomes essential. When you train your mind to persevere under pressure, your ability to rally in any situation will serve you well.

Before you bail, reach for technique.

Sometimes tension in a room can be intimidating, especially when ideas get challenged around the conference table. Before shutting down, apply this systematic approach: Recall your two words of strength (recite them to yourself), move your coffee cup three inches to the right, take up space, then throw in a strong gesture and confidently proceed.

Nothing destroys credibility like wimpy words.

Impart credibility with careful word selection. Wimpy words weaken your message. Phrases such as "I think, I feel, or I believe" drain your credibility. After an entire presentation of weak language, your perceived uncertainty will leave us questioning your knowledge of the topic and ultimately your influence in the room.

Turning Speaker's Anxiety into Powerful Presentations

Announcing your anxiety only amplifies it.

Under no circumstances would I recommend disclosing to your audience that you are nervous or unaccustomed to speaking before a particular number of people. Calling attention to anxiety often intensifies your body's response to it and will magnify any weakness to your audience. Instead, let it energize the room. See lesson 35.

Being comfortable means taking a nap.

My clients often ask me to help them become more "comfortable" on stage. However, comfortable does not equal confidence. In fact, quite the opposite. Comfort is fuzzy slippers and a warm blanket. Confidence will come when we consciously tap into our personal strengths and actions. Remember your two words.

What is on the other side?

The "Hump of Anxiety" is a bell curve. Anticipatory anxiety (just anticipating speaking) will increase dramatically up the left side of the curve, peaking at the top when you start to speak, then falling off as you hit your stride. Knowing what is waiting for you on the "other side" is the key to staying strong over the top.

25

Turn nervous energy into positive energy.

Speaker's anxiety produces nervous energy that we often wish wasn't there, but without it, we'd be too relaxed! Who wants to listen to a lazy speaker? Think of this energy as a reminder that you're not at home in your slippers, but in fact, about to do something important. Energy equals passion. Control it and let it keep you sharp.

Find your strategy for personal fortitude.

You will need a strategy in the beginning to get you over the hump and into your smooth sailing zone. This will differ for everyone, however, imagery can be a useful technique, especially when it's used consistently. You're basically training your brain to equate one particular image with strength, fortitude and success.

Think less about how to "impress."

When we worry about "impressing" our audience, we begin the downward spiral of self-inspection as our mind wanders off on an internal dialogue of self-judgment. This is an example of how our ego can obstruct us and pull us out of the present moment.

38

Think more about how to "express."

When we begin to effortlessly "express" ourselves without second-guessing our next move, we reach the most sought-after zone of self-expression. Authentic expression is a freedom to reflect and express all that we are, and all that we have to say. When we think of ourselves less, there is no ego constraining us, and our ability to communicate becomes boundless.

One person is waiting for this.

Communicate your message with confidence knowing that everyone has a story that needs to be heard. This is your gift to your audience. Overcoming anxiety can be as simple as remembering that your story is unique, and if it touches just one person in your audience, you have succeeded.

Every success follows you on stage.

With every success you gain the confidence to take on even greater challenges and keep adding to your book of wins. Put every win in your back pocket. (See lesson 5.) Anchor on a past excellence and let it drive you (smiling) though to your next success. Visualize yourself winning!

Visualize: Go from stress to strength.

When the unexpected happens (a projector fails or your presentation didn't save properly) remind yourself to go from stress to strength by practicing visualization techniques. Just as we can imagine an athlete, moments before a competition, freeing their mind from all external stress, we can learn to acquire this same skill when the going gets tough.

Using Strength at the Negotiating Table

Negotiation is not always a conflict.

Unfortunately, many people will remember an interaction involving a conflict longer than one without. Because of this, there is a tendency to avoid these situations. However, there's great satisfaction in strategic problem solving, and if we can walk into a negotiation with the mindset that we are there to solve a problem we will have much better results.

Lead with your strength, always, always.

If you cannot identify your strength, your ability to negotiate will suffer. (Refer back to lesson 1) The unique talent and expertise that you bring to the table will become most helpful during a negotiation. When you pull power from authentic strength, you become a more credible and convincing source of information.

Enjoying the process delivers better results.

Your mood can directly affect the course of a negotiation, so it's important to pay attention to it. An "incidental emotion" is one that stems from an unrelated earlier event, but will influence your emotions at the negotiating table. Creating a positive mindset will go a long way toward achieving the result you want.

Confidentiality can be your secret weapon.

Former U.S. Secretary of State, Madeleine Albright, was quoted as saying: "Negotiations are like mushrooms, they are more likely to thrive in the dark... outside the spotlight of public scrutiny." Sometimes a fishbowl negotiation with everyone watching is not advantageous. There will be times when discussions between parties need to be kept confidential to have a desirable outcome.

46

Negotiate with the future in mind.

Okay, so you won the negotiation, but at what cost? If you've "won," but at the expense of another, you can bet they'll always remember that. It's important to negotiate a successful outcome for both parties. Keep the future in mind throughout the process and consider how "taking the hard line" will affect future relationships, and perhaps your company's reputation.

Flip the dialogue in your head.

A successful negotiation starts before you walk in the room. Preparation is critical. Consider how you're going to approach the situation. You may find you need to flip your internal dialogue from "What's in it for me?" to "What's in it for them?" This "flip" will help you appreciate what the other side needs to gain, and tailor your conversation.

Just ask, or you'll never know.

At a company I worked for in Atlanta, one of the sales managers would walk through his department and loudly remind everyone: "If you don't ask, you don't get!" I can still hear him now, and I've always remembered that phrase anytime I hesitate to ask a question.

Relationships don't always prevent hardball negotiations.

The power of a strong relationship can often contribute to a smooth negotiation. However, it's wise to be prepared for a "ninth inning zinger" you didn't expect. Sometimes without warning, the players can change and disrupt an established dynamic. Solid preparation beforehand will give you the confidence to keep the discussion moving smoothly.

50

Cultivate the capacity to say no.

Don't be afraid to say no. It takes great strength to walk away; it is not a weakness. There may come a time when your resolve and perseverance are not wise actions. Be mindful of when you need to cut your losses. Take time to consider your values while remaining strong in your convictions. (See lesson 100.)

Take Time for Mindful Decision Making

The dangers and deceptions of multitasking

"Hire more multitaskers!" Not today. What was once considered a desirable trait and a cost-effective hire, is simply not true, research now shows. Our brains are not wired to multitask. Instead, we end up jumping from one thing to another (switch-tasking), often never completing the first task, decreasing our overall effectiveness and productivity.

Dedicate the time to build awareness.

Find an activity that heightens your senses. Pay attention how long it takes you to enter "the zone" and what creates an inspiring environment for you. (Notice I didn't say relaxing, see lesson 33.) Comfort is great for naps, but we're looking for a deliberate mindfulness that comes from achieving a focused state of awareness on the task at hand.

53

Hey, whose deadline is this anyway?

Don't get caught up in what other people think is urgent. There will always be deadlines looming, however it's perfectly reasonable (and wise) to take time to think things over. Communicate the fact that you need time to consider all the options and that you will respond by the end of the week with a decision.

The dangerous demise of think-time.

The demise of "think-time" in a hurried work environment has produced poor and sometimes reckless decisions. With too much emphasis on speed, shortcuts are taken, teams are not consulted, and snap judgments are made. When pressure is high and deadlines threaten, remember that all bad decisions will eventually surface. Time saved now is not worth the trouble later.

Successful people utilize the morning hours.

Time is the most valuable thing you have. What if you utilized the quiet morning hours for the activities you value the most? Make a list of how you're spending your time now and where you'd like to spend your time. It will soon become obvious what is getting ignored. Now you know how to spend those morning hours!

Heighten attention and get fully present.

Become mindful in all things, even small things. There's a great story about the legendary basketball coach John Wooden and how he taught his players to put on socks. One wrinkle in a sock could lead to a blister, which could affect the entire game! When you get fully present, and start with the small things, great things can happen.

Don't just react, learn to interact.

Read any article today about the impact of social media, and you'll discover that we're all losing our ability to interact in person with others. Certainly this is concerning for businesses when the time comes to make decisions. Are executives merely reacting to a situation without mindful interaction? Next time, consider whether meeting in person would yield better decisions.

Disconnect to gain greater mental clarity.

Just changing your physical location can help get your head in the game. A ten-minute walk can clear your mind. When you return, focus your attention on the task at hand and allow yourself at least thirty minutes to settle into a state of flow without outside distractions. Once you've reached flow, stay with it for as long as possible.

Your decisions reflect who you are.

Because decision making is a cognitive process, it would follow that it would also be a mindful process. But in the age of "deal with it as quickly as possible and move on," we have to question how many decisions genuinely reflect our principles. Remember that every decision you make has your personal stamp on it. Be deliberate!

Know the consequences of bad decisions.

The costs and consequences of a single hurried decision can have a long lasting impact. A rush judgment to save time can cost a company millions over the long haul. If you're fortunate enough to be in a position to make decisions for your company, take time to evaluate all your choices in order to better navigate complex issues.

Owning your Power with Authority Figures

Knowing yourself is your strongest defense.

When communicating with authority figures, self-knowledge is power. Know who you are and what you believe in, and be prepared to communicate that. Stay in alignment with your principles and have strong confidence in yourself and your experience. (See lesson 8.)

Be aware of changing power dynamics.

Power dynamics exist throughout our personal and professional lives. Use your keen sense of intuition to assess the balance of power in the room and be on the lookout for power shifts that can derail a meeting. Look for intimidation techniques, and watch out for a disruption of power when someone new enters the room.

Your knowledge and experience is unique.

Critical, yet easily forgotten: You bring a unique background and thought process to everything you do. So much more than your resume, you are a glorious combination of everyone who has touched your life. Sometimes all it takes to own your power is to think of someone remarkable who has had an impact on your life, and channel their influence.

64

Belief versus Truth, what's the difference?

What are your beliefs, and what are your truths? Unfortunately, what we're told by others (often authority figures) tend to become our beliefs. Ask yourself, are they facts or universal truths? If not, learn to reclaim your power by rejecting those beliefs that have been holding you back and creating a false reality.

"Power is like being a lady...

...if you have to tell people you are, you aren't." That's a quote from Margaret Thatcher, former British Prime Minister. Certainly power is about the ability to influence, however it is not something that is wielded over people. Communicating a sincere passion around the work you do often results in the power to make a lasting impact and affect change.

66

We are our own toughest critic.

Sometimes our toughest critics are in our head. We think: "What am I doing here? I'm going to get found out!" Referred to as the Imposter Syndrome, these feelings typically surface during an evaluative or stressful encounter, often when sharing ideas with authority figures. The key is to think of yourself less, and express more. (See lessons 37 and 38.)

Responding to "What do you do?"

Ah, the innocuous question with the standard robotic response! We've all answered it enough times, but when asked by someone in a position of power, it can feel intimidating. Instead of falling back on your title (I'm a product manager) find your "wow factor!" Get creative and think of ways you can stir up interest in what you do.

Learn the art of self-promotion.

When studying Polarity Management, you will find a harmonious, yet contradictory loop of humility versus arrogance. In this model, if looked at singularly, neither is great for business. But when looked at through the polarity flow, they can exist together in a balanced relationship. We should think about self-promotion through this dynamic model.

69

Push past comfort, push past fear.

One of my swimming idols is Lewis Pugh, who wrote a book called *21 Yaks and a Speedo.* In chapter 8, titled *Push,* Lewis reminds us that sometimes we give people with authority too much power and we can get tangled up in red tape, preventing us from "achieving our impossible." We must "Push Past No!" Read the book!

70

Strength is built from day one.

Win or lose, every experience builds on the last and shapes the person you are today. From struggle emerges great strength. Over time, your true character is built and cannot be shaken by anyone else's opinion of you. Your authentic strength lies within.

Embrace the Storm, Motivation will Follow

Understanding the metaphor of the storm.

The storm is a metaphor for disruption and chaos. Why do we need a metaphor? Because metaphors can often teach us things at a deeper level, yet we can refer to them easily because they tend to be quite simple. In this case, "There's a storm rolling in," and it can motivate us to take action.

There will always be a storm.

Life is like that, there will always be disruption. Sometimes we seek it, and sometimes it is thrust upon us. But either way, when we stay in a state of mental security, there is little risk and also little gain. Stay curious, be courageous, and embrace the storm!

Take on your most demanding tasks.

When the storm hits (and it will) think to yourself: "How can I use this moment to propel me forward? How can I use it to challenge me in ways that I haven't been tested before?" Instead of choosing to "hunker down," what if you took this opportunity to take on your most demanding tasks?

77

"Oh poor me" is not strong.

"Poor me" sits on the couch and complains about their situation without taking action. If your job has pushed you into a "poor me" situation, it is time to leave (and fast). My favorite Teddy Roosevelt quote sums up this situation quite nicely: "The worst of all fears is the fear of living." What have you done today?

75

Flip your response, flip the outcome.

Consider your typical reaction to stress. Is it helpful? Now think about how you might "flip" your response next time you're faced with a difficult situation. It will require a mindful intent. Instead of focusing on the negative, reflect on what you have gained throughout the total experience and be grateful for the opportunity.

Anger is a powerful motivating force.

A positive attitude has plenty of advantages, however there is an upside to anger. Anger can work as an unexpected motivating force that propels us forward when we least expect it. Sometimes all it takes is a mental stimulant to push us through a plateau and achieve something great. Take advantage of these moments.

There is always room for humor.

Abraham Lincoln said: "Were it not for my little jokes, I could not bear the burdens of this office." The power of humor is undeniable in many situations, and quite often (especially during a storm) we all need a bit of humor. I have certainly gotten through many challenges in my life with "my little jokes."

And another one bites the dust.

The difference between success and failure can often come down to the ability to rally. When the going gets tough, someone needs to bring people together and generate enthusiasm (to rally!) Those who lack the capacity to rise to the occasion will find that it's easier to give up or go through the motions instead of putting forth extra effort.

We do it for the rush!

The rush of a challenge. The thrill of an experience. Ask anyone who has competed in an athletic event why they did it, and you'll often get these responses. Win or lose, it's the thrill of the total experience. When a business opportunity doesn't work out, consider the whole experience and what you've gained from simply participating.

From your struggle emerges irreplaceable fortitude.

If you could visualize fortitude, what would it look like? I recently visited the Normandy D-Day beaches and swam from Omaha Beach towards Utah Beach. As I was swimming, I visualized fortitude. Before I left, I picked up a smooth rock from the water which now sits on my desk as a constant reminder of strength, bravery and courage.

Push Yourself Toward your Breakout Plan

Get up, break out, move up.

Is your comfort zone limiting you? What would you do if you were not afraid to push those boundaries? Whether it's a new position, a new job, or a total life change, you will need a breakout plan that evaluates both risk and opportunity. Plan for success, give it your all, and always integrate a backup strategy.

Don't wait any longer to change.

Today is the day to make plans, set goals and hold yourself accountable. Write down a 30, 60 and 90-day plan and log your progress. Review your log every few weeks and look for trends and patterns. Pay attention to overused phrases ("I'm exhausted!") that could reveal how you're feeling and what needs to change, (Get more sleep!)

83

Small increments can make great gains.

When your goals are large, break them down into small (and sometimes atypical) daily changes. A year before I set off to swim the English Channel I washed my face with cold water every morning. I imagined it was the great North Sea! That simple act prepared me mentally for my daily cold-water training sessions.

84

Excuses are barriers to your success.

The mind can race through thousands of thoughts per day, many of them the same as yesterday, and a very large percentage are barrier-thoughts: thoughts that contain excuses to hold you back. But all you need is one thought, one reason to push yourself. Find that reason and then say to yourself, "If I don't do it, I'll never know!"

Ego is limiting. Let it go.

When we don't ask for help, it's usually because of ego or pride. The fact is, no one gets to where they are today without help from others along the way. Trash the "I am an island" mentality, and acknowledge the fact that there is no weakness in accepting support and advice from others. Their experience builds on yours.

With strength, all things are easier.

"To begin, begin." -William Wordsworth. To get started, try a journal app on your phone. Each morning it will ask you to list a few things you will do (actions!) to make that day great. Then in the evening you reflect back on what happened throughout the day because of those actions. With results comes strength to continue.

Being comfortable does not equal promotions.

You might be comfortable being a heads-down worker, but this will not get you noticed or promoted. Pushing yourself toward your breakout plan will require some uncomfortable moments. A breakout plan is a risk, and will include unpredictable and unforeseen events. Acknowledgement of the unknown will help you move forward.

Remember: your knowledge is your strength.

Don't confuse expert power with positional power. Expert power stays with you, while positional power is connected to your position at work. Expert power is your expertise. This is your strength, and this will travel with you to your next job. But positional power is fleeting and should not be confused with your true knowledge.

89

Will power is how we continue.

Sometimes it's hard to continue when faced with challenges. But what would happen if you gave up too soon? While mountain biking with friends, several cyclists turned around before reaching the top and were not rewarded with "the view." "What about the view?" is now my metaphor for will power. It's how we keep going and keep pressing on.

The human spirit has no limitations.

Your work does not define you. Nor does it confine you. Every experience has a ripple effect. The people we meet along the way and the experiences we gain all create our expanding network. These circles spread out and can have a significant impact in our lives going forward.

Strong Leadership for a Greater Purpose

Inspire others: Your legacy is waiting.

Be bold and do good work. If you follow these two simple rules, you will most certainly be rewarded with the honor and privilege of inspiring others. Your inspiration becomes a legacy, and that is worth living for. Pay attention and prioritize what is important.

Provide a strong foothold for others.

If I could select one guiding principle of leadership, it would be this lesson: (paraphrased from Confucius) "As we seek to establish ourselves, find a foothold for others. As we desire attainment for ourselves, help others to attain." If we all followed this principle, what great things would happen?

Seek opportunities to be a mentor.

Most of what we learn about leadership is learned outside of school. If you have attained a leadership position, consider how you might give back to your community by becoming a mentor. Of all the ways to invest your time, becoming a mentor can have a significant impact on everyone involved. There is something to be learned from everyone.

Acknowledgement can be your greatest asset.

Set an example for strong leadership by spreading the gift of acknowledgment to others. It is a universal human need that is often ignored in our hurried world. Combined with the appropriate level of interpersonal skills, executive presence, and genuine appreciation of others, acknowledgement can be your greatest asset.

Leaders earn respect by respecting others.

What type of leader are you? Do you command respect, or earn respect? Obviously, the one who can roll up their sleeves and get to work will earn more respect than the leader who falls back on her title and dictates what needs to get done. Mutual respect goes a long way towards the ultimate success of the team.

Connect the dots and give back.

Be generous! The greatest gift you can give yourself and others is to connect the dots that map to your current success. Where did you get your start? Who inspired you? Who helped you along the way? Answer these three questions and you will find an opportunity to give back.

Bring strength to your greater purpose.

When you have strength, use it for a greater good. After you've found your strength and pushed the boundaries of your own comfort zone, now it's time to take it to work and share it with the broader community. To truly use your strength for a greater purpose, find ways that it can benefit others.

Match your power with your purpose.

Business fortitude is something that is gained over time as we develop a deeper understanding of our authentic strengths, and how we can match them with a greater purpose. When we put our power behind a broader purpose, our strength of convictions becomes clear. Quoting the wisdom of Lewis Pugh once again: "When you've got purpose, everything becomes possible."

99

Align your goals with your passion.

What does it take to get the job done? My best advice is to fully understand who you are, and then ask yourself if your next venture matches your personal brand. If your answer is "Absolutely, Yes!" then jump in and do it. When our goals match our passion, the result becomes an authentic reflection of our work and dedication.

100

Always be strong in your convictions.

It is all possible with strength. Be unshakeable. Know who you are and stand by that always. You will win and lose friends along the way, but you will always remain true to yourself. In the end, this is the most important.

About the *Six-Word Lessons Series*

Legend has it that Ernest Hemingway was challenged to write a story using only six words. He responded with the story, "For sale: baby shoes, never worn." The story tickles the imagination. Why were the shoes never worn? The answers are left up to the reader's imagination.

This style of writing has a number of aliases: postcard fiction, flash fiction, and micro fiction. Lonnie Pacelli was introduced to this concept in 2009 by a friend, and started thinking about how this extreme brevity could apply to today's communication culture of text messages, tweets and Facebook posts. He wrote the first book, *Six-Word Lessons for Project Managers*, then started helping other authors write and publish their own books in the series.

The books all have six-word chapters with six-word lesson titles, each followed by a one-page description. They can be written by entrepreneurs who want to promote their businesses, or anyone with a message to share.

See the entire *Six-Word Lessons Series* at 6wordlessons.com

Made in the USA
Middletown, DE
03 March 2023

25928558R00076